Internal Recruitment

Getting The Basics Right

By Paul Myers

Introduction

This book is a must read for Recruiters, Recruitment Managers, HR Professionals and Operational Leaders / Hiring Managers or anyone else who is involved in the recruitment process.

The book will take you through the basics of the recruitment journey, focusing on the key steps where everyone's getting it wrong.

The focus is not to teach you how to source candidates, or what you need to do, to do it effectively. Anyone can source candidates thanks to the internet. There are many books, online training courses and lots of sourcing events that are available for anyone who wants to learn how to source effectively.

Artificial Intelligence is a big thing in recruitment now. Lots of people are talking about it yet no-one really knows enough about it, to use it effectively. Most tools that claim to use AI are simply using advanced algorithms to match keywords, skills and experience and there's an argument to say that it's not actually AI at all. We won't even be touching on this as we need to get the basics right first.

So, what are we all getting wrong? I believe we're all getting the core of recruiting, you know, the important stuff like business and market knowledge, vacancy briefings, candidate communication and management, recruitment process management, interviews etc wrong!

If you don't believe me, just log in to LinkedIn and view the numerous updates complaining about recruiters and companies providing pretty poor candidate experiences throughout the process.

If you're a recruiter, this book should jog your memory and remind you what you should be doing and make you a better recruiter in the long term. If you're a recruitment leader or HR Manager, it might help you to remember what you should be doing to create better candidate experiences and will help you make sure that your recruiters are effective in their roles. If you're an operations leader, a hiring manager, or anyone else who gets involved in the recruitment process, you'll learn what recruiters should be doing to support your hiring needs, what you should be doing to support them, and what you should be doing to contribute to your company's success in hiring talent.

I've was thinking about writing this book with dose of humour, unfortunately I've been told my jokes are pretty rubbish, so I didn't bother. I also admit to swearing too much and as such, there is some bad language, if you can't cope with the occasional F-Bomb, then this isn't the book for you.

The book hasn't been proofread by a professional writer or editor (so apologies in advance for any spelling and grammar mistakes), it's self-published, it comes straight from my experience, my thoughts and is written in the way I like to talk; so you'll either love it or hate it!

I hope the book challenges you to think about the areas of recruitment where companies have become lazy and I hope it will also help you stop being robotic; instead, focusing on helping you and your team to start thinking and acting like humans during what is arguably one of the most human focused areas of business, recruitment.

Why?

It's a question I asked myself and thought about deeply before writing this book. I wasn't sure it was even a good idea, there's lots of recruitment books out there that have been written by individuals with more experience than myself.

I did a bit of research, I even bought a few books and I realised, everything seems to focus so much on candidate sourcing (which let's face it, is probably the easiest part) and how to react to different recruitment situations in a transactional manner.

I think something's missing and that's why I've written this book. Rather than teaching you how to react to situations, I'd like to get you thinking and acting in a way that will enhance efficiency and performance throughout your recruitment cycle.

You'll be introduced to NOIB*ing*; a method of understanding how to analyse, think and act upon any situation. I was introduced to NOIB*ing* by the indomitable Jean-Christophe Baudais who is the inventor of this methodology. Together we have developed a series of masters within the application that helps recruiters, HR and hiring managers learn how to think and act, rather than react, on any situation that can occur within the recruitment lifecycle. But, enough about that, I haven't written this book in order to sell a tool.

JC is an individual I have worked with in the past, delivering leadership training within a global business before working in partnership with him in other scenarios. Despite him being French and myself being English, we connected from the beginning and we're still friends and partners in business some 6 years later, he's also partly to blame for me writing this book, so if it's complete bollocks and you feel you've wasted your money, blame him!

Finally,

Recruitment is easy isn't it? Anyone can do it, and many do, yet apparently, most people are a bit shit at doing it, especially according to everyone who doesn't recruit. Recruiters manage to screw up recruitment and are the most incompetent workers on the planet if you believe everything you read on the internet. It appears companies haven't yet figured out how to do recruitment properly, so who's to blame for this? In some cases it's the recruiters, in some cases it's HR, sometimes it comes down to the hiring manager. In short, it can be you, me and anyone else involved in the recruitment process.

If you could fix one thing about your recruitment process, what would it be?

Contents:

1. Business Knowledge – You Know Your Business, Right?
2. Acquiring Market Knowledge
3. Vacancy Briefings
4. Job Advertising
5. Working with External Recruiters
6. Effective Pre-Screening Calls
7. Interviews – The Horror of it All

8   Recruitment Reports To?
9   Turf Wars!
10 Close
11 Thank You
12 Finally

Business Knowledge – You Know Your Business, Right?

You know your business, right? If you are involved in any part of your company's hiring process you must know your business before you start any hiring activities. It makes sense doesn't it? All too often, recruiters and sometimes HR Managers, even operational employees involved in recruitment, do not have enough knowledge about the wider business they are recruiting for.

A common mistake made by many companies is assuming that their recruiters and hiring managers, know the business and do not require any training or learning materials. Quite often, new joiners to a business get the usual induction with a few company presentations and introductions, but thereafter, what education do they get? Too often, they're left to get on with things and all they know is their role, what they do and where they sit in a wider business.

Think about the impact this has in terms of both candidate attraction and engagement and the trust and relationships between recruiters and hiring managers.

A recruiter is usually a candidate's first glimpse of the company. If they can't explain what your business does, nor get excited about your company, how can they sell the role in a way that's going to engage and make a candidate enthusiastic about the opportunity. The truth is they won't, and you really should question whether they are representing your business appropriately.

The same goes for hiring managers and anyone else involved in the hiring process. Imagine the recruiter has done a great job of selling the opportunity to a candidate. The candidate arrives for an interview and there's your hiring manager, full of enthusiasm about his department, team and what is does, but then he/she offers no information or, is unable to answer questions about the wider business.

It's not enough to communicate with potential candidates and simply regurgitate information that can be found on your company website such as your much publicised 'Company Culture'. Candidates want to know more than the standard corporate bullshit, they want inside information and they want to hear it in person, from real people.

How do you ensure your hiring team knows your business?

You invest more time in their induction and their knowledge acquisition.

There is an exercise for internal recruitment teams I use when building internal recruitment functions, I call it the 'Business Knowledge Project' (ok, so its name is a bit obvious and potentially uninspiring perhaps you can help me think of some snazzy title to dress it up a bit). The exercise can be used for both new and experienced recruiters. You should consider using it for HR professionals, Line Managers, and general employees (it could be particularly useful for salespeople) in future as part of a more interactive induction process – now there's a smart idea perhaps we'll talk about that another time.

So, what's involved in this exciting project you ask?

The recruiter / recruitment team is presented with an exercise in which they need to obtain information about the business they are working for.

After gathering information, they then must build a presentation based on the initial key areas in which they were required to obtain information, and they are asked to present it back to key stakeholders and hiring managers.

Once the recruiter / recruitment team have presented to key stakeholders and hiring managers, they then must present to each other internally (although if you're smart enough, you might set aside a half day or day of presentations with the whole team present).

It's important that you ensure the recruiter / recruitment team structures their approach to this task.

NOIB – Need, Organise, Involve, Benefit

What does the recruiter **Need** to know? It's a good idea for them to sit down and document everything they think they need to know about the business. They should at least be able to come up with the following:

1. What does the business do?
2. What are the key products and services?
3. What are the different internal and external business units and teams?
4. What is the organisational structure of the business units and teams they are responsible for?

5. Who are the key stakeholders and hiring managers for their business?
6. What are the roles within the teams and what do they do?
7. What is the culture of individual teams / business units / business?
8. What are the top selling points of the team / business unit / business?

This is by no means an exhaustive list, but it covers the basics. If your recruiters are not even covering the basics, you must question their interest in your business!

Once they have the list of what they Need to know, they then need to think about how they **Organise** themselves and the information they are going to obtain:

1. Where?
    a. Company website?
    b. Intranet?
    c. Stakeholders, Hiring Managers, Employees, HR?
2. How?
    a. Downloading information off the internet/intranet?
    b. Asking internal people to send information?

- c. Arranging meetings with internal people to discuss?
3. When?
    - a. When is the deadline?
    - b. When can they get the information by?
    - c. When can they complete their presentation?

If the recruiter thinks about the task in this way, they will be able to better manage their time which will help them learn more, retain information, and deliver a better presentation.

The recruiter / recruitment team now also need to focus on who they need to **Involve** in the task at hand:

1. Who is going to provide the information?
    - a. Key Stakeholders?
    - b. Hiring Managers?
    - c. HR?
    - d. Finance?
    - e. Other employees?
2. Who is going to document the information?

You should insist that the recruiter / recruitment team members must fulfil this task within a specific timeframe (you can decide on this, but generally a week is a decent amount of time).

What is the **Benefit** of doing this?

The level and depth of knowledge gained, shows you whether your recruiters/recruitment team have an interest in your business. If they show an interest in your business, they are likely to be more passionate about it when describing it to candidates.

Through actively researching your business, talking to the people in it and learning directly from them, it gives the recruiter / recruitment team a far better learning experience than the 'here's our company presentation, everything you need to know is in there' approach.

Giving the recruiters / recruitment team an opportunity to learn from key stakeholders and hiring managers expertise, helps them understand and retain the information they've gathered much better.

It creates trust and builds better working relationships between the recruiters and hiring managers because the hiring manager then has confidence the recruiter / recruitment team understands their business.

Candidates get a much better experience, the recruiter / recruitment team can share much more valuable information and the knowledge they have enables them to speak to candidates with credibility.

It creates a better working practice for sharing of information internally within the team. It enhances each recruiters' knowledge of the whole business, eliminating the silo effect whereby a recruiter knows everything about their division but nothing about the rest of the business. It creates better business continuity by creating an environment where a team of recruiters are able to manage any absence or holidays or unexpected long-term leave of absence with confidence, due to their understanding of the complete business.

This is a collaborative learning approach which can also bring benefits to your whole business (especially if there are new managers), as recruiters, HR professionals and hiring managers and key stakeholders can all take part in the task. It enhances relationships and business knowledge, and it will increase their effectiveness and performance when describing the company to candidates, providing the candidates a better understanding of whether your business may be right for them.

<u>Acquiring Market Knowledge</u>

Now that your hiring team understands your business, they also need to understand the market your business competes and operates in. Candidates working within your target market will expect your hiring team to have a good knowledge about the market they're working in. If for example you're hiring within the tech industry, your team will be expected to know about technologies and trends within it. Other points you team should be aware of are, key competitors, salary and benefit benchmarks and general market conditions, particularly at a more senior level.

Time and time again you can see complaints on social networks, about recruiters who are lacking knowledge or have very little experience in the market they're hiring for. Candidates are all too quick to raise this as an issue and it can reflect badly on your business.

Your recruiters and hiring managers must have an overview and knowledge of up to date and relevant information about the market you operate within to speak credibly with potential new hires. If you've recently brought on a recruiter who doesn't have experience in your market, you must give them time to learn about it, otherwise, you're setting them up to fail rather than setting them up for success.

How do you ensure your recruiters know the market?

Give your recruiters the appropriate amount of time to research and find the relevant information. They can in fact do this in parallel with the 'Business Knowledge Challenge'.

The exercise I use for this is called (wait for it) …. the 'Market Knowledge Project' (Another inspiring project name I know, but hey, it's more about the content of the task and the benefits it brings, right?). Again, you can use this exercise you can use for both new and experienced recruiters and if you're smart, you'll also use it for HR professionals, Line Managers, and general employees

So, what do the recruiters do?

The recruiter / recruitment team is asked to obtain market information related to the market the business they are working for sits in, both geographically and industry wise and they set about this task following the same 'NOIB' structure as used in the previous exercise.

What does the recruiter **Need** to know? They should at least be able to come up with the following:

  a. What market / markets does the business operate in?
  b. Which countries does the business operate in?
  c. What are the demographics of labour in the regions in which the company wants to attract employees?
      a. Labour availability and skills
      b. General / Average pay and conditions, comp & bens
  d. Who are your direct competitors in the markets your business operates in?
      a. What is their position and reputation?
      b. What do they offer?
  e. What other competition is there in the regions your business operates in?
  f. What are the key networks and social channels for the market and regions in which your business operates in?

g. What are the specialist / local job boards in the market and regions your business operates in?
h. What industry bodies can be contacted about opportunities for networking and advertising?
i. What are key universities and alumni that are present in the market and regions your business operates in?
j. What trade shows and events take place that could potentially be hunting grounds for talent?

I'm not saying the above list is the gospel according to Paul, it really does cover just the basics, but if well thought out and researched, it will arm your recruiters with powerful knowledge and information.

Now they need to **Organise** themselves and the information they are going to obtain:

4. Where?
    a. Competitor websites?
    b. Industry websites?
    c. Labour office?
    d. Industry networks, forums, books or other publications?

- e. Job boards?
- f. Internal employees?
5. How?
    - a. Downloading information off the internet/intranet?
    - b. Asking external/internal people to send information?
    - c. Arranging meetings with external/internal people to discuss?
6. When?
    - a. When is the deadline?
    - b. When can they get the information by?
    - c. When can they complete their presentation?

The recruiter / recruitment team now also need to focus on who they need to **Involve** in the task at hand:

3. Who is going to provide the information?
    - a. External people in industry? Who?
    - b. Internal Team Members (HINT: sales & marketing/business development might be a good team/group of contacts to talk about the industry/market don't you think)?

c. Internal Recruitment Colleagues (If you set this task as a group, then they can all work together and spread the key tasks between them, deciding who does what; if they organise themselves effectively that is)?

I don't like to set a short timeline for this task as there is lots of information to gather and it can take a while to really know your market. For example, I would set this as a target for completion by the end of the 1st quarter. I know that ideally you already wanted your recruiters to be up and running yesterday. It can be started in tandem with the Business Knowledge exercise, but I wouldn't set a week as a target for completion. I would also set either quarterly or bi-annual state of the market reviews, in order to ensure your recruiters, maintain an up to date knowledge of the market.

What is the **Benefit** of doing this?

The level and depth of knowledge gained, shows you whether your recruiters/recruitment team have an interest in the market your business operates in, they will be able to engage better with candidates.

Through actively researching your markets, talking to the people in it and learning directly from them, it gives the recruiter / recruitment team a far better learning experience and provides your business with some competitive analysis and general market information that can help you make business decisions in other areas, not just recruitment.

Your recruiters obtain a better all-round knowledge and sometimes even a competitive advantage when trying to engage with potential new hires. Through understanding elements such as local conditions, employers and direct competition, they can then understand your company's USP's and use these both in attraction and engagement of candidates.

It further creates trust and builds better working relationships between the recruiters and hiring managers because the recruiter in fact becomes an advisor / consultant to the business, demonstrating market knowledge to help set the right level of expectation and managing those expectations more successfully.

Vacancy Briefings

My favourite part of the recruitment process is the vacancy briefing, or intake meeting as some people call it. For me, it's the most crucial part of the overall recruitment process. So much so, I'd go so far as to state that if your recruiters and hiring managers (yes that's right, both parties are responsible for the success of this stage), are not prepared to put enough effort in at this point, then you might as well say, fuck the rest of the recruitment process!

This is your recruiter('s) and hiring manager's best chance to ensure they are fully aligned regarding their understanding of the role, the requirements and setting the right level of expectations for each other. It's the part of the process where both parties really begin to build a relationship and it can also help in building a working partnership whereby both parties are taking responsibility for the hiring process.

The information shared in a vacancy briefing should enhance the attraction and sourcing strategy as well as the management of the overall recruitment process. If neither side are willing to invest their time in holding an effective vacancy briefing, then you're not going to be very successful in hiring talent. I can't put it any simpler than that.

How to facilitate a successful vacancy briefing:

Think about what the recruiter needs at this point?

Job description?

Name of the hiring manager?

If they've got this information then that's great, we're off to a good start.

But what if they don't have a job description? Well I'm afraid that's just shitty practice and you shouldn't be allowing any vacancy to be approved without there being a job description for it. Even worse than that, you or your hiring manager want an individual to come in and make the job their own, therefore creating their own job description, that's bullshit too. You're being lazy. You have an idea of what you want, so document it and use it as a basis for hiring. At least you can amend it with what the reality of the role becomes as you go alone.

Your recruiter is also not responsible for writing the job description. The hiring manager is (perhaps with some help from HR). The vacancy briefing is not an excuse for getting help to write a job description. It wastes time for both your recruiter and hiring manager. Without at least basic job descriptions, you're going to fail, make sure you provide this most basic of requirements to your recruiters.

Let's assume that you have a vacancy request from a hiring manager which has passed through an approval process and the notification along with the job description has been sent to the recruiter.

The recruiter sets up a meeting with the hiring manager. They're going to plan for the meeting, aren't they? AREN'T THEY!?

We can look at what the recruiter **Needs** to know by breaking it down into categories:

1. General Information
2. Understanding the role
3. Required skills, experience and education
4. Understanding the right fit
5. Selling the opportunity
6. Candidate Attraction & Sourcing
7. Setting the Expectations

General Information

All recruiters should be able to understand the most basic information. I would expect a recruiter to focus on getting the following information:

- Job Title
- Type of contract
- Length/Type of Contract
- Location (Office/Home/Split/Multiple Locations)
- Working hours (flexitime?)
- Reporting to (Direct / Matrix? Who?)
- Compensation Package (Base salary + variable)
- How the Commission / Bonus Structure works
- Benefits
- Relocation Package / Visa Support
- How urgent is this position?
- Why is this position urgent?

Now, this all seems fairly basic however, amazingly, I've had vacancy briefings with recruiters of large companies (because I was not allowed direct access to the hiring manager; we'll talk more about that in the working with recruitment agencies chapter), who had no clue about commission and bonus structures, or stated they would need to get back to me about the benefits package. Imagine that when you've got to try and sell a sales role to a salesperson and you can't even talk to them properly about how the commission structure works – yeah, good luck with that one!

Understanding the role

Most recruiters have rarely worked in some of the positions they are recruiting for, so you can't expect them to really have a full understanding of the position and what's involved, can you? Well yes you can. If your hiring manager is fully engaged and wants to invest time in ensuring the recruiter understands the role, and you have a recruiter who is engaged in your business and wants to learn, then this part formulates a general understanding that enables a recruiter to advertise effectively and also talk to potential candidates with credibility.

I would suggest that your recruiters should really be covering the following as a minimum:

- What will this person typically do daily?
- What other tasks are involved?
- What interesting projects will this person work on?
- Who will this person interact / communicate with across the business?

- What is the size of the team where do they fit in to this?
- What are the short- & long-term objectives for this role?
- What outcomes / impact will the person performing this role have?
- What difficulties might someone in this role face?
- Who can I talk to in your team that is already performing / has performed this role?

Imagine your recruiter confidently being able to give all this information to a candidate without even being asked. What sort of impression do you think that would make? Even if the candidate had to ask, if your recruiter had this information, it would still create a good impression.

It's great to ask to sit with someone already doing the role, if it is not a completely new role for the business. As well as the hiring manager's grand overview of the position, your recruiter can pick up the reality of the role from the person in post. Obviously, you need to be careful with this, if you're looking to replace someone in the position, you don't really want your recruiter talking to that individual, especially if there are issues with performance or attitude.

Think about why it is so important for the recruiter to understand the role. What impact do you think it has, when a candidate has a conversation with one of your recruiters and they get fobbed off with statements such as; "Obviously I don't need to tell you what you'll be doing as you've already got a lot of experience in this area, I'd like to focus on….." or even worse, and I have personally heard this one a few times; "I'll send you the job description so that you can see what you'll actually be doing".

Required skills, experience and education

It should be clear that a set of skills and experience are required. In some cases, it takes some work in understanding and sometimes, negotiating on the recruiter's behalf, to separate what's essential and what's nice to have.

It's good to ask questions that make the hiring manager think before they answer, your recruiters will get far better information and a much better understanding of the real requirements:

- What information do you expect to see in a candidate's CV and my pre-screening feedback and what key experiences / situations must someone have / have encountered, to be considered for this role?
- What are the critical skills someone needs to be able to demonstrate, for you to see they could be successful in this role?

- There's never a perfect fit, what skills and experience can we negotiate on (must have's vs nice to have's)?
- What education / qualifications are necessary? Why are they necessary?

Ok, so there's not many questions in this part, but that's the point. Asked in the right way, these questions will encourage a discussion that will provide far more information than just asking what skills someone needs to have.

These are critical questions that must be answered as the recruiter will most likely (and in fact should) set a part of their sourcing strategy and pre-screening interviews around the requirements that are clarified in this part of the conversation. It will help them close in on the right candidates rather than simply checking for buzzwords within the candidate's CV/Resumé.

It will enable the recruiter to structure better questions for their pre-screening interviews, leading to a better understanding and feedback, regarding the candidates' suitability for the role. The hiring manager will have a much better insight, enabling them to focus on key areas during the next interview.

Understanding the right fit

I'm still amazed at the number of companies and recruiters who adopt a completely one-sided process when it comes to understanding whether someone 'fits.

There are some companies that like to hire based on their 'company culture'. There's other that have core values. In both scenarios, I find that the company is only ever looking to see if the candidate matches their culture or shares their values. I've rarely seen a company that cares about whether their culture and values fit the candidate. I'm not saying it should be completely focused on the candidate, but both parties need to understand if it's right for them.

Your corporate culture is bullshit!

I strongly believe that if you are hiring based on culture, and you're a large, international organisation, it can't be done on a company-wide level. Values can be instilled across a business (generally because it is an agreed way of doing things that can be replicated across teams in the business), culture is built at the individual team level. The people, their personalities and quirkiness build the relationships and culture within each team. Whilst your finance team may share the same values as your sales team, do you really believe they have the same culture? I don't....

There are organisations, start-up, medium and large enterprises, where management try to impose a culture upon their people. I've worked in environments where this has been the case and ultimately, even when management has brought in consultants and cultural specialists, the business continued to suffer, even to the point of failure. In these scenarios, the people – those that nearly every business claim are its 'most important asset' are often unhappy and don't stay in the business for long

Agree or disagree, I don't really care, but hopefully it makes you think about things a little differently.

If you insist on hiring for cultural fit, make sure it's a fit with the team culture and that the team's culture fits the individual you'd like to hire.

It's important both your hiring manager and recruiter understand how to do this, and I've given you a few tips below on what questions your recruiter should ask during the vacancy briefing:

- Tell me about your other team members, what are they like?
- How would you describe your team's culture?
- What type of person do you think will fit within the team?
- Why do you think that?

- How would you describe your leadership style?
- What personality traits would you like your new team member to have?
- What other attributes or working attitude do you like your team members to have (regarding time, proactivity, adaptability, flexibility, willingness to learn etc)?

Asking questions like these not only give your recruiters a great understanding of what the hiring manager is looking for, it gives them a greater understanding of the hiring manager themselves and enables recruiters to really give candidates a clear vision of the team, it's team members, and what it will be like to work with the hiring manager. Notice I didn't say 'work for', it's important your recruiters describe working with rather than working for when discussing team members and hiring managers. They work for the business; they work with people.

Candidates have over the years, have increasingly placed more importance on their need to know about their colleagues and manager. It's that 'cultural fit' thing that I ranted about earlier. They're looking on sites like Glassdoor, to check out reviews and feedback on businesses, it's important that they feel there's a potential match for them.

Selling the opportunity

At a point in time where the unemployment rate across Europe is at the lowest levels we have seen in many years, your recruiters have to be able to sell your job opportunities, particularly for example, if you're looking for technical profiles such as software engineers.

Software engineers, particularly senior engineers, are a hot commodity. Times have changed in recent years. Smart recruiters and companies realise they no longer choose the engineer, the engineer now chooses them. They have become accustomed to the fact they have to sell their opportunities. It's simply not true that the market is dead, that no-one is available. The fact is that most software engineers are open to hearing about new opportunities, but for that engineer to choose you, you must make your offer compelling.

In addition to the information your recruiter has already gathered, they need to understand how to sell the opportunity. I've given you some examples below (sticking with the software engineer theme) that could help your recruiters become more successful when selling the opportunity:

- Why should someone join your team and work with you for your business?

- How would you describe the purpose of the products / applications / services your team delivers?
- How would you sell this role if you were looking for candidates yourself?
- What attracted the current / past team members currently / previously working in this role? Is that still valid now?
- What can a new joiner expect in the first week, month, 2 months, 3 months?
- What technologies and tools are available / used now and in future?
- What methodologies are used in your team (Agile, Scrum, Waterfall) and what projects might they be working on?
- What opportunities do they have for professional development and learning and what is their potential career progression?
- What do you and your team members enjoy about working in the team / business?

Of course, not all candidates have the same needs and desires when considering who to work for. You won't always be able to catch the attention of everyone, but investing time in thinking about and answering some of the questions above, or perhaps other questions that may be relevant in helping you sell the opportunity, could just make the difference in someone choosing whether to join you or not.

Candidate Attraction and Sourcing

When it comes to candidate attraction and sourcing, it's an opportunity for the hiring manager and the recruiter to really work as a team to build a strategy for advertising, networking and proactive sourcing.

The recruiter should have a decent market knowledge right, Afterall, they've done the market knowledge exercise haven't they?

If they have, they'll have already looked at where similar jobs are advertised and who's advertising, knowing where your competitors are and what else they do. The recruiter should be able to at least demonstrate which job boards and social networks he/she intends to advertise on along with where and how he/she intends to source candidates.

The recruiter should however want to cover all avenues and the following questions are examples of simple questions that should engage the hiring manager and get them thinking about it too, giving them partial responsibility for the success of the attraction and sourcing:

- Have you asked for any referrals from your team? Are you willing to? If not, why not?
- Where would you or your team members search for jobs like this and what search terms would you use?

- Where does our target audience hang-out? What industry groups and networks do you and your team recommend I look at, for opportunities to advertise and network?
- Where else do you think we might have some attraction and sourcing opportunities?
- Where did you find your last hire?
- Are there any specific competitors you feel might have the type of candidates we're looking for, that I could actively headhunt from?
- If we struggle to find candidates, which recruitment agencies would you recommend?

Attracting and sourcing candidates is paramaount to your success in hiring. Without candidates, you have nothing. Surveys suggest that up to 90% of employees, are open to looking at new opportunities. Not all of those people are actively looking, some are generally satisfied, but if something better comes a long they'd be happy to hear about it.

With this in mind, your recruiter needs a attraction and sourcing stratgy that will cover both the active and passive candidates in a given market.

Ultimately the recruiter is responsible for the attraction and sourcing strategy but, your hiring manager and their team members are potentially able to provide an insight to industry networks, events and other potential sources that your recruiters may not be aware of.

The more opportunities they have regarding where to look, where to post, where to actively engage with potential candidates, the more likely it is they will have success in finding talent for your business.

Setting the expectations

When it comes to setting the expectations within a vacancy briefing, it a question of both sides being willing to negotiate, agree and make commitments to each other.

The recruiter should set the hiring managers' expectations with realistic timeframes for the delivery of qualified candidates. It's important to set extremely realistic expectations during this process and let the hiring manager know when the recruiter expects to begin phone screens, and when they can most likely expect to start receiving candidate profiles with recruiter feedback. It's also important to let them know what a realistic number of applicants for the type of role they are recruiting for would be. The recrutier should slso let them know what a realistic number of applicants for this type of role would be. Remember, the recruiter is the expert in sourcing and attracting candidates. They have the recruitment lifecycle experience and understand that candidates do not magically appear just because a job is posted.

The recruitment process should be discussed and agreed during the vacancy briefing. Allow for flexibility in your recruitment process in order to run a quick and efficient process (We'll cover this in another chapter later). The recruiter and hiring manager should agree on:

Timeline for feedback on resumés / profiles submitted
Timeline for scheduling of interviews
Designated interviewers and back-up interviewers
Timeline for feedback after interviews
Timeline for providing offer following succesful interviews

It's important to be understand as a hiring manager, that if the role is urgent, then the hiring manager needs to show a sense of urgency when it comes to taking part in the hiring process.

Recruiter „How urgent is this position?"
Hiring Manager „Very urgent, we need someone as soon as possible becuse we can't finish a project for our client"
Recruiter „So if I were to provide you with 3 qualified candidates by the end of the week, when would you be available to interview them?"
Hiring Manager „Maybe in 3 weeks....."

Think about it, how should the recruiter feel about this. The recruiter has been asked to find canidates quickly, advises that they can find some by the end of the week, but the hiring will not commit to moving through the process quickly....do you think it's likely the rest of the recruitment process is going to be a success.

Feedback is important too, it's not just about committing to attending interviews, it's also about provide effective communication and unfortunately, this tends to be one of the areas in which company's fall down most often.

Recruiter „Hi Jean-Christoph, did you get a chance to review those candidate profiles I sent you"
Hiring Manager „Oh hi Paul, Err, not yet no, I've been really busy lately, I'll do it for you by the end of the week...."
Recruiter „Hi Jean-Christoph, it's me again, I don't wish to be a pain, but last week you said you'd provide me with feedback on the candidates I sent you. I haven't heard from you yet, do you think you could look at them today for me?
Hiring Manager „I'm really sorry Paul, I'll come back to you by the end of the day...."
Candidate „Hi Paul, I was just wondering if you had any feedback from the hiring manager yet?"
Recruiter „ Hi Jitka, Thanks for getting in touch, I've been in touch with the hiring manager this morning and they've advised they will come back to me at the end of the day."

Candidate „Hi Paul, just following up on our communication earlier today, did you get feedback from the hiring manager?"

Recruiter „Hi Jean-Christoph, Are you available to discuss feedback on the candidate profiles, the candidates are waiting for feedback."

Hiring Manager.....................

Recruiter „Hi Jitka, I'm afraid I haven't got feedback for you yet, I can only apologise, I'm sure something came up, I'll chase this again for you tomorrow."

Candidate „Hi Paul, Ok, well just to let you know, I've just been contacted about another role and have an interview booked already for tomorrow, if you hear anything let me know."

Recruiter „Hi Jitka, Ok, please keep me updated, I will try to get feedback as soon as possible for you."

Recruiter „Hi Jean-Christoph, Could you please give me feedback on the candidate profiles sent to you today, the candidates have other opportunities that they are starting to move ahead with and I wouldn't want you to lose out on them."

Hiring Manager „Dear Sender, Thank you for your mail, I am currently on annual leave for the next two weeks........."

This is unfortunately a very familiar story to many recruiters. The candidate experience in this scenario is extremely poor, and your recruiter is wasting his/her efforts.

Imagine what a candidate must feel if they've attended an interview with the hiring manager and they are waiting for feedback. It's a period of both fear and excitement for them, and you do this:

Hiring Manager "Thanks for coming today Jitka, it was great to meet you, we'll be in touch shortly to give you feedback."
Recruiter "Hi Jitka, I just wanted to follow up with you to see how you think the interview went and what your thoughts are at this stage?"
Candidate "Hi Paul, I think it went ok, they asked a lot of technical questions but nothing I think I didn't handle well. I'm quite excited about the opportunity. As you know, I have two other opportunities but this one is my favourite so far. It would be interesting to see what Jean-Christoph thinks about me, I really can't tell if he liked me."
Recruiter "Great, thanks for the feedback Jitka, I'm sure it went fine. I'm due to speak with Jean-Christophe in the morning, so as soon as I have done so, I will call you to give you feedback."
Candidate "Great, thanks Paul, I look forward to hearing from you."
Recruiter "Hi Jean-Christoph, can you let me know when we can chat today regarding Jitka who you met at yesterday's interview? She says we're her favourite opportunity and I'd like to wrap things up if possible so that we don't risk missing out on her."
Hiring Manager "Hi Paul, Sure, I'm busy up till 10, I'll call you after then."
Recruiter "HI Jean-Christoph, I'm sure you must have been held up in a meeting or something, can we rearrange please?"

Hiring Manager………………..
Recruiter "ring, ring, ring, ring, ring, ring, ring, click…..Hello, you have reached the voicemail for Jean-Christoph, please leave me a message…….."
Candidate "Hi Paul, do you have any news for me?"
Recruiter "Hi Jitka, I'm afraid it looks like the hiring manager got caught up, I'll come back to you as soon as possible."

Another week passes by……

Recruiter "Hi Jean-Christoph, what's the feedback for Jitka who you recently interviewed?"
Hiring Manager "Hi Paul, Sorry for not coming back to you sooner, it's been a really busy time. Regarding Jitka, I loved her, she's smart, knows out technology and she'd fit right in, can you make her an offer? I'll send you the details in an email"
Recruiter "Great news, I'll get hold of Jitka asap to make the offer and I'll let you know if she accepts."
Recruiter "Hi Jitka, sorry for the delay in coming back to you, I'd like to discuss an offer of employment with you, when would it be a good time to call?"
Candidate "Hi Paul, Thanks for your mail, unfortunately as I hadn't heard anything from you, I decided to accept an offer with ……."

There really is no reason for this to happen. It's inexcusable. Unfortunately, it does happen. Your recruiters bear the brunt of candidate frustrations and are the ones who are targeted with ridicule about the unprofessionalism of recruiters. Commitment from the hiring manager to attend interviews, provide timely feedback and play and active part in your recruitment process all helps with both the efficiency and success if your recruitment activities, along with creating a great candidate experience.

Personally, I like to negotiate a number of other commitments too. As a recruiter, if you've demonstrated that you've fully understood the hiring manager's requirements you should be in a position where the hiring manager trusts you to skip the resumé / profile review stage and go straight to interview however, this can take time and only comes about once you have earned the hiring managers trust.

A good way to test the level of trust would be to ask the following question:

If I was to find a candidate interested in the opportunity who met the requirements we've agreed on today, I assume you'll have no concerns about me scheduling an interview for you with that candidate?

If the the hiring manager doesn't agree with this, you need to find out why, what are the objections to this. Once you understand those objections, you can often overcome them by demonstrating what you will do and how it will benefit the hiring manager.

If the hiring manager agrees, that's great, give yourself a pat on the back, you've just cut down future time spent on your hiring process, you can look forward to skipping the hiring manager resumé / profile review stage and going straight to interviews.

Focusing on communication, your recruiters and hiring managers should also agree on the regularity of updates. I would recommend a weekly update. Even if there's no new candidates, the recruiter should at least update regarding their recruiting activities for the open role and what has happened to date.

Extra tips

To avoid rushing through the vacancy briefing, I like to call the hiring manager, or pop round to see them if we're in the same location, to advise I want to set up the vacancy briefing and arrange a suitable time. I agree on the day and time, and then send them a meeting request accordingly.

Within that meeting request, I provide instruction on what we will cover, and I attach a template vacancy briefing document with all the questions I'd like to ask them during the vacancy briefing. I ask them to review the document and have a think about those questions in advance.

The reason I do this, is because from time to time, you'll come across a hiring manager who is highly engaged and wants to really help in recruiting talent to his/her team.

I've had hiring managers who have filled in the document and sent it back to me prior to the vacancy briefing. This is fantastic, because I can then run a preliminary search based on their responses and come to the meeting with some profiles to review there and then with them, getting even more of an understanding of what they really like.

On other occasions, hiring managers have brought the completed document with them to the meeting, we've clarified all the points accordingly, and then set about running some searches together.

In both instances, it creates much more value from the vacancy briefings.

Additionally, if you do this for positions where you're going to engage a recruitment agency rather than work on the role yourself, having all this documented and sending it to the agent along with the job description, before they come for a briefing, saves both the agent and the hiring manager valuable time (we'll cover working with agencies in another chapter too).

Job Advertising

I really didn't want to write about job advertising, but I feel compelled to do so, because it will help me get a few things off my chest and will allow for some good opportunities to swear!

Most corporate job adverts are fucking boring, BORING!

Bland headings, paragraphs of corporate bullshit bragging about "we are this, we are that, aren't we fucking amazing", endless bullet points copied and pasted from poorly written job descriptions, and more often than not, a list of requirements as long as your arm.

Many recruitment agency job adverts aren't much better either, how many of them start with "My/Our client is……" or "We are looking for……"

My pet hate is that sentence at the bottom of some adverts; "Successful candidates will be contacted within two weeks of applying". If there was ever a statement that basically said, "if we think your shit, we're not going to contact you and if we think you might be good, we'll get round to contacting you at some point when it's convenient for us" …….my god!

Now I don't want to tarnish everyone with the same brush, because there are some great adverts out there, written by people who understand how to engage with their target audience through written word. Unfortunately, there's a lot more crappier adverts than good adverts, produced by individuals who would rather throw shit at a fan hoping it sticks, rather than spending an hour of their time writing a better ad. By the way, the latter of these are generally those who will then complain there's no candidates, we all know that's not true don't we?

There lots of advice out there on the internet about how to write job adverts, lots of different articles and blogs that tell you to do it this way or that way. It can be confusing. I'm going to offer some short pieces of advice based on what has worked for me.

Understanding your Audience

Do you understand what your audience wants to see in a job advert? Lots of marketeers think they know their audience, but the moment comms and marketing gets a hold of responsibility for the formatting of your job advertising you can kiss goodbye to posting adverts that really attract candidates (unless of course you're a company like Google or Apple who have hundreds of applications per position, just because of the brand status).

You want the reader to think "This sounds good. This is perfect for me. I want to learn more about this position". Forget about all the information online telling you what different types of candidates want to see, the only way to really your target audience is to ask them.

It's an easy step, if you're hiring software developers, go and talk to the software developers already working at your company. Ask them what type of job advert would stand out to them, ask them what information is important in a job advert, ask them how it should be structured, how should it speak to them.

I recently worked with a software development team who needed to hire a web designer. We did this exercise together as a group. The team members confirmed what they wanted to see on a job advert was the following information:

- Title
- Short piece of information about the company, what it does and its history
- What is/are the project/s and what's cool about it
- What's the Tech stack
- Why they should join and what they will do
- Salary

Now that's interesting isn't it? There's no mention of benefits on their list. Job boards tell you that you should include your benefits on the job advert, so I raised the question why it wasn't on their list. The answer was that the benefits were not important, they wanted a reason why, they wanted to know what impact they would have by doing what they would be doing.

I went away, wrote a new job advert and showed it to them... success, every one of them said they would apply to that advert. I took it to comms and marketing and (I'd like to say that after some negotiation, but really it was persuasion), managed to get it accepted. The business had a preferred format and a corporate standard and here I was, telling them that the standard adverts did not attract our target audience and we needed to change it. I showed both the standard version and the new version of the adverts and advised them of feedback from our own software developers.

The result: Success. Previous advertising for the web designer had generated a total number of candidates that you could count on one hand, even if you had two fingers missing! The new advert generated more than 40 candidates out of which we were able to select the very best for interviews and offers.

The example above was just one situation, you need to think carefully about your target audience. Go and talk to them about their self-interests and what would appeal to them within a job advert. There's no 'one size fits all' method to job advertising. Your message to finance candidates is likely to be very different to your message to sales candidates.

Job Advert Titles

A job advertisement must grab the attention of a potential candidate. All job boards list job adverts by job titles and it's the first thing a potential candidate sees. Depending on the job board you're posting on, you're quite often limited in terms of the amount of characters you can use in your heading. This may partly be to blame for the pages and pages of jobs with the same title, but it's mainly down to you and your creativity.

I did a search on a job board which shall remain nameless, for Java Developers. There were over 350 jobs. I looked at the first 100 jobs and 96 of them all had the title 'Java Developer'. The 4 jobs that were different didn't have inspiring titles, they stood out only because they were different.

You need to do more to grab attention! But what should you do?

Well how about simply jazzing it up a little bit?

Let's say you're working for a company that is developing new tech for the energy industry, the vision being to create a more sustainable, cost effective and greener energy supply that would directly impact our carbon footprint.

Would you dare to use something like the following?

JAVA DEVELOPER – SAVE THE PLANET!

It's a killer title for a job advert… it will stand out on that page of Java Developer job adverts for sure.

Get creative, titles on job adverts don't have to be boring. They can be fun, different, and engaging. Just think about your business, product, industry, and your target audience, think about how you're going to make title of your job advert stand out from the rest.

Interesting content

It is essential to keep the potential customers interested in the advertisement. This means large amounts of dull text just are not going to cut it, for example; You can start the body of your advert with a question. Why?

Well, in the same way your brain has just told you to think about why; a potential candidate will naturally want to answer a question when they see it in front of them. We're programmed that way. Our subconscious tells us to answer the question. What a great way to engage with your potential candidates.

I'll stick with my Web designer who's going to save the planet!

Example Question: How would you use your web design skills to develop a user interface for an online platform, that will be used potentially by millions of people globally, creating a smarter, more efficient method of distributing energy, reducing our carbon footprint, and positively impacting the environment?

You'll notice, it's a question that will make someone think. It's not a closed question with a simple yes or no answer, although these are perfectly fine too if you want to be more direct.

Example Question: Are you someone who cares about the environment and would like to use your web design skills, to provide a cool user interface for a web platform that provides better energy solutions, reducing our carbon footprint?

If you don't want to use a question, then a short, original, entertaining and informative paragraph about your company, it's vision and what it offers is another good way to start. I'd like to emphasise the fact it should remain short.

Example: We are company XZY, a purpose driven company focused on significantly impacting the 'Energy Trilemma' by facilitating a transition to affordable, reliable and clean energy. With strong investor backing, we're a start-up that has grown from our humble beginnings in 2016 to a team of almost 100 people across four European locations. Our exceptionally talented team is made up of a diverse group of brilliant minds from the fields of engineering, physics, mathematics and software development; who challenge and solve real world problems, developing some of the most sophisticated technical solutions in the energy market.

That's enough! You do not need 2 or 3 paragraphs of text about your company blah blah blah, candidates will read all that when they visit your website. It's short, concise, it tells the reader who the company is, what it does and its history in just six and a half lines.

Describing the job

Job adverts with a copy and pasted list of responsibilities are just bloody awful. They're dull and boring. I'd want to know more about what I'm going to be doing, and according to research, so do today's job seekers. I don't want to see a list of what I'm responsible for, especially when the job description will confirm that later…. Ah, and there it is, the biggest problem in job advertising!

If you're one of those companies that is using job descriptions as a template for advertising, allowing your recruiters to simply upload or copy and paste, then you're getting it wrong. Your job advert is supposed to create desire to join you, and you think an uninspiring list of responsibilities and requirements is going to do that? Good luck with that!

I like to describe why someone should join and what they will do into one section. The successful advert I mentioned above had the following:

Why you should join:

- You'll join a small international and multicultural team of 12, in which every single team member has a direct and high impact on our results.
- You will have ownership of designing the UI of our new web application.
- Working in an Agile/Scrum environment, you'll be collaborating with web coders, and developers to create excellent web design.
- You'll be exploring new ways to create a technically accurate application that is fun to use for millions of people globally.

You, You, You, You, YOU. It's a powerful word, it speaks to the individual, it personalises this list and makes it more exciting, interested candidates connect with this far more than to a list of responsibilities.

Your requirements

Of course, you want to make it clear that you have some expectations regarding the requirements of the role. But instead of simply listing key technologies or experiences, try making it more appealing to.

Try to describe your requirements as more of an opportunity for potential candidates to use their capabilities and enjoy doing it.

Instead of requirements, I call this section 'About You'. Again, it's more personal and speaks to the individual. I then further utilise 'you' statements to keep it focused on the individual:

- You understand the boundaries of web-based applications and really enjoy designing both beautiful and responsive UI that has a positive impact on the user.
- You love working with Adobe Photoshop or other similar graphic editing software such as Affinity. Although not important, you may even have some exposure to HTML and CSS.
- You enjoy teaching others how to pay attention to the visual part of the product.

- You are curious and passionate about web design; you keep yourself up to date on the latest trends and emerging technologies

The great thing about writing your requirements in this way, is that potential candidates will either relate and connect to this, they will subconsciously say 'yes I do understand', 'yes I love working with', 'yes I enjoy teaching', 'yes I am' or, they will disassociate themselves from the opportunity, which is fine, you don't want those people anyway!

Call to action

I mentioned earlier my pet hate regarding how adverts are closed off by some companies. There's a case for putting in the hiring process within a job advert if you wish, although it isn't something I'd say is an absolute must.

What every job advert must have though, is a call to action. People need to be persuaded to apply. Hopefully the content of your job advert has achieved this, but just to make sure, sign off with an impactful statement telling your target audience to apply.

Again, I'll go back to my Web Developer who's going to save the planet.

This role offers you a great opportunity to have an impact on the environment globally, and you will genuinely see the results of your efforts. Click the 'Apply' button today!

Make sure it's clear how to apply. On most job boards there is a button which applicants can click to apply. If you want to give them alternative methods, then leave your phone number and email address in the body of the advert.

TIP: Put your recruiters on a recruitment copywriting course. It's easy to tell the difference between adverts written by a recruiter who understands recruitment copywriting and a recruiter who is copy and pasting from job descriptions.

Working with External Recruiters

Love them or hate them, external recruiters are here to stay. There are of course different types of recruitment agencies and we'll take a brief look at them now.

Contingency recruitment agencies

Contingency recruitment agencies work on a risk and reward model, which means they only collect a fee from their clients once a qualified candidate who has been searched and placed by them for the position in question, starts in the role.

Due to the higher level of risk involved for contingent recruiters, with the possibility of not getting guaranteed commission for their efforts, multiple competitors most likely to be working on the same open vacancies, even competing with the client who has advertised the role; contingent recruiters are often motivated to put candidates forward to a company more quickly than other recruiters in order to try to get a higher fill rate.

This might sound appealing, faster delivery however, it is often not the case. Contingent recruiters are often working on several similar positions that are required by many clients and push the same candidates forward to each client in the hope that one of those clients will move quickly and increase their chances of a placement. They are forced to work quickly and the quality of service and work is not always of a high standard.

Most contingent recruitment agencies work on entry level or unqualified positions, and you'll find that many of these agencies have recruiters who have little recruitment experience, often combined with a lack of market knowledge and a very transactional mindset regarding recruitment.

It's not all bad though, some contingency recruiters work on an exclusive basis. This means the recruiter has the role with your company exclusively and can spend more time on providing a quality services and delivering better results.

Retained Recruitment Agencies

Retained recruitment agencies differ from contingency recruitment agencies in that they are generally more professional and charge a fee for service rather than a fee for success. They get paid for the work they put in, as well as the result.

The approach to recruitment is vastly different. They will actively headhunt, tapping into passive networks as well as searching through their active candidate database.

Typically, the client will pay a percentage of the expected fee up front then another payment when the shortlist is produced; and then the final balance on success. The first payments are not refundable should the client cancel the role.

The benefit to you as a client in working this way is you get 100% commitment. It strengthens the relationship as the two parties work together to produce the outcome required within appropriately agreed timeframes as opposed to 'find me someone as quickly as possible'.

A recruiter working on a retained basis will take time to source appropriate candidates which will ultimately mean a better-quality result at the end of the process.

Selecting which agencies to work with

It can be tempting to go out to multiple agencies to try and cover the market however, in today's employment market, with skills shortages and low unemployment rates, this just isn't effective.

More often than not it leads to candidate ownerships issues with agencies fighting over the same pool of candidates in a given region.

Take time to think about what roles you are recruiting for. A recruitment agency might claim to be a specialist in the field in which you are looking for candidates, but do the recruiters working for them really know your market?

Check them out, invite agency recruiters to meet with you and ask for examples of their personal success in your market, find out how long they've been with their current employer and how well their performing against their own KPI's. Get information on which clients they've worked with in your industry and what roles they have successfully filled. Be sure to check out their understanding of your market and find out what they know about you.

Tip: Beware of any recruiter that comes to a meeting with you, without any knowledge of your business and has not researched your company, they're a complete waste of time. If they haven't done the basics of researching your business, how can you trust them to do a proper job and successfully provide you with top quality candidates.

Agency Fees

For those of you looking to save costs on agency recruitment, skip this section!

I don't often negotiate on price when engaging with a recruitment agency. I try not to, because I have learnt over many years, the level of service varies greatly dependent on the conditions agreed with the agency.

If they're a contingency recruitment consultant, they'll most likely have other clients willing to pay the full rate, and guess where they're going to put their efforts? I don't need to tell you, do I?

You might get lucky if you offer a role on exclusivity or demonstrate that there will be a long term partnership with them, but don't try pulling their pants down, knocking them down from 20% to 17.5% is enough to keep them interested. 15% you're pushing your luck, any lower and you might as well call up all the tinpot recruitment agencies happy to work on 10%. There's a reason why they're happy to work at 10% and it's not because they're good at what they do!

If the external recruitment provider is a retained search consultant, for me, it's simply not negotiable, they are experienced professionals who are good at what they do and for the value they add to my efforts and the business, it's worth the money. These generally good enough at what they do, to be able to pick and choose who they work with rather than vice versa. In fact, in all the roles where I have worked internally, I can probably count on one hand, the number of times I have been cold called by a retained recruiter.

Preferred supplier lists (PSL's)

Oh, the big corporates love a preferred supplier list, don't they?

I'm going to keep this simple. PSL's, don't bother, waste of fucking time!

Let's say you're one of those big corporates. The aim of your PSL has never been to create a level playing field across all providers, improving the quality of service provided. If it was, you wouldn't implement 1st, 2nd or 3rd tier suppliers.

Let's face it, if you've gone through your 1st tier suppliers and they couldn't help, it's either a very difficult role to fill and you probably need to enlist the help of a retained recruiter, or they're simply not very good and you need to review your selection criteria for recruitment suppliers. If it's first scenario, what makes you think your 2nd and 3rd tier suppliers are going to do any better?

A good recruiter knows when your PSL is not performing, because they know the market, they track your company and your positions because they like to be able to share competitor information with their clients, and they see all those positions that have been open for 6 months and more.

Funny thing is, when they call you to discuss the potential of supplying talent to you, even if they can demonstrate success in hiring for those roles that both you and they know are open, the WoD (Wall of Denial) suddenly drops down from the heavens. You're happy with your PSL and you're not looking to work with additional suppliers.

Undeterred, that recruiter who's not on your PSL is smart, they find a couple of profiles and through their expert researching skills, they find out who the hiring manager is and get in touch to discuss the profiles. The hiring manager is quite excited, he/she hasn't received any profiles from your PSL agencies and here is his/her knight in shining armour. The hiring manager tells the recruiter your company has a PSL but copies you in on an email where they ask the recruiter to build a relationship with you…. Silence…. You're not going to contact them because you have a PSL.

Well done. Pat yourself on the back. You've created additional angst for your hiring manager, you've also prevented potentially suitable candidates from getting a new role, and the recruiter has decided that because you refuse to engage with them as a client, they're going to headhunt from your company instead.

Another reason the quality of service rarely improves, is because a PSL is implemented with a clear aim to drive down your recruitment costs. The big corporates believe that they are doing recruitment agencies a favour by allowing them to have the prestige of sitting on their PSL for a reduced rate.

The funny thing is, the not so good agencies believe it is a privilege and can't wait to receive all those roles the massive internal recruitment team has already worked on for the last 4 weeks.

The fact of the matter is, the good recruitment agencies don't want to be on your PSL. They charge a premium for their service because they know they're good at what they do, and they're working successfully with your competitors whilst your PSL are scrambling around for leftovers!

A final point I am going to touch on is that many PSL's are set up with the idea of having a group of providers that can cover all their needs. This is just nonsense. It's nonsense because you do not find contingency agencies that are good at recruiting across the whole corporate spectrum at all levels. So invariably, the PSL fails and when it comes to the 6 month or yearly review, they're given a poor performance rating and after another 6 months without any increase in performance, you're left to review your supplier list once again.

Unfortunately, with the power of the procurement function and finance combined, it's often not possible to get away from building a PSL. I know this, because I have done it twice however, I was smart enough to recognise that external providers we were selecting might not be able to cover everything and therefore, I looked at specialist agencies for different areas of the business, and reserved the right to go to retained agencies for senior or hard to find, specialist appointments outside of the PSL when I knew it was a role likely to be beyond their capability..

Basic keys to success with recruitment agencies

Your external recruitment providers should not be treated like a pizza delivery service. You can't just place an order and expect to receive it in an hour. You must build a relationship and work in partnership with your chosen external recruiters; here's how you can make it a success.

Vacancy Briefings

Once you've agreed to work with an external provider, giving them as much information about the roles you want them to help you with is essential. Give your external recruiters the information they need about the role and help them to prepare for vacancy briefings. Give them direct access to the hiring manager.

You remember the vacancy briefing document I talked about in a previous chapter? Well if you've managed to get a hiring manager to complete that document or if you yourself have completed it following your own vacancy briefing, send it to the external recruiter before you meet with them. it's worth it.

I have sent this document to an external recruiter and invited them to come and meet both myself and the hiring manager to discuss the position.

The recruiter came along with his sourcer and his company CEO and upon arrival and after a warm introduction, the first thing the external agency commented on was the quality of the information we had provided them. They were amazed that 1. A vacancy Briefing Document so detailed had been developed and 2. That a hiring manager had actually taken the time to complete the form. It was "The best vacancy briefing document I've ever seen, and it really helped us understand your needs".

Now of course, the CEO was laying on the charm and also waiting for his opportunity to pitch his company, and the recruiter was pitching himself, demonstrating his market knowledge and understanding of the position and the requirements, and the sourcer, well the sourcer was just there for the experience :). The meeting was short, professional but also open and, I honestly believe the external providers were surprised and weren't just blowing smoke up our arses. Why? Well, because they came well prepared, they demonstrated a good understanding of our business, the role and the hiring manager's needs. They were attentive, they listened, they made it clear what their strategy for fulfilling our needs was, negotiation was quick and easy, and we were receiving relevant profiles within hours....

I do not understand companies who do not give external recruiters the information they need, to be successful at hiring for the role. In some cases it honestly believe, internal recruiters view them as a threat and therefor, would rather the agency fail, in order to be able to come back to hiring management and be able to say, "see, I told you there was no-one available".

I understand that giving direct access to hiring managers is not always possible in every business, but wherever it is possible, you absolutely must give your external recruiters direct access to them at the vacancy briefing stage. It doesn't have to be face to face, it can be video conference, at worst it can be a telephone call, but I would not accept e-mail as a suitable communication channel for the most important part of the recruitment process.
As an internal recruiter, you know what you need from the hiring manager to be successful. Guess what, an external recruiter needs the same.

Communication

Communication with external recruitment agencies needs to be regular and if you get it right, they help you manage the whole process with the candidates far better.

In the same way you should be communicating with direct candidates in a timely and professional manner, you should be communicating with your external recruitment suppliers when they are working on roles for you.

Whether you give them direct access to the hiring manager throughout the process, or whether you channel all communication through the recruiter, your external recruiter needs regular updates and for you to act, because they are managing the candidate's expectations. Ultimately, if the external recruiter is not able to provide feedback and information to their candidates, it's not the external recruiter that takes the blame or is the focus of discontent, it's you and your company.

Poor communication with your external recruiter leads to two challenges for you moving forward.

1. Candidates who received a poor experience in your recruitment process, are likely to not want to apply for your roles in the future, meaning you are depleting your potential talent pool.
2. The external recruiter having had a bad experience and covering your market as their specialist area, is most likely working with your competitors and will focus on your organisation as a potential pool of candidates

3. Having given a bad experience, you now also probably need to find a new recruitment supplier

I realise that's three challenges; I was just testing if you're still reading and paying attention!

Building relationships

You really must build relationships with your external recruitment agencies and their recruiters. By doing so, it enables an agency to have a better understanding of your business and this extremely valuable.

If you have a good working relationship with someone that understands your business, that you can count on time and time again, it becomes a pleasure to cooperate and the quality of service is always better.

If your external recruiter wants to come for coffee now and then to discuss roles, or just the partnership, or wants to try and sell you another service, let them come and meet you (although you'll want to manage how often).

Get to know them, because in the future, they might be interested in working with you as an employee, they might be important in helping you with your future too…. Ooh HR Managers are gonna love me for that one!

Job Offers

I'd like to believe that for every recruiter, the moment of glory is being able to make the offer of employment to a candidate and having them accept the offer (but there is always one wierdo, who's got to be different).

When it comes to making offers of employment to candidates supplied by an external recruiter, I think who makes the offer of employment, depends on their level of involvement in the recruitment process.

If your external recruiter has been supporting you with making interview arrangements, providing feedback, following up and making arrangements for further steps and keeping the candidate interested in your opportunity throughout the process, providing you feedback on the candidates likeliness to accept an offer of employment, then let them have the glory. Discuss the offer with them, put it in written form to avoid any mistakes, and let them make the offer to the candidate.

If your external recruiter merely provided a sourcing and pre-screening service, and you have managed the process thereafter, then enjoy the glory of making an offer of employment yourself.

Say thank you

It's amazing how many companies forget to say thank you to their external recruiters for their service.

I don't know if this is just bad manners or something that they do on purpose, but let's face it, even though you've paid for a service, the external recruiter through fulfilling your requirements, has solved a need. They've helped your business and they've taken some pressure off, and they've also delivered exactly what you wanted.

Let's go back to the pizza delivery service, you make an order, it's delivered in under an hour, the pizza boy or girl hands over your pizza and you hand over your cash. Then what do you say? You say thank you and goodbye. Well I do anyway, if you're someone who doesn't, then I just think your fucking rude!

Say thanks!

Effective Pre-Screening Calls

Some companies call them pre-screening calls, some companies call them telephone interviews, either way it just sounds so formal, I like to call them Initial Conversations and as such, invite candidates to have an 'initial conversation' with me about the opportunity.

I do this, because I don't want my potential candidate to be nervous on this call, I want to have a two way conversation to help them find out if the role I have matches their skills and experience, their needs and motivations and what they want in a new role. I also want to find out the candidate matches our needs.

Straight away that may well be confusing to some of you. Especially those of you in large corporate companies. Why would I say that? Well I say it because in most cases, in a larger corporate environment, it's quite often a one-way, pre-scripted telephone interview processes that focus purely on the candidate's skills and experience, competencies and salary expectations.

Recruiting is a bit like dating, for there to be a match, both parties must be interested in each other.

I generally find that smaller companies, and start-ups, are much more open and better at looking at it this way.

I used to work in large corporates where competency-based questions were used during telephone interviews and I thought this was the way it must be done. After 12-13 years of doing things more or less the same way (I can't remember exactly, as I get older I forget more and more of my past) I then worked for a much smaller company where I was taught to engage with candidates in a different way during telephone interviews.

I've had far more success since then, providing quality candidates to the businesses I have been working within. I want to share this with you as I believe it really will bring you far greater success in hiring talent.

Getting prepared for the initial conversation

Let's do some NOIB*ing* to get make sure we're prepared for our initial conversations with candidates

Slightly different to the NOIB*ing* we did earlier, we need to look at the **Facts**, what **Actions** we will need to take, how we will **Engage,** and then visualise the **Benefits**.

So, how do we do it? Well first off, let's consider the facts:

- First and foremost, we want to be sure we're not going to be wasting our time; is the candidate worth talking to?
- Do you have time in our calendar to schedule calls and have you scheduled time?
- Have you scheduled time with the candidate?
- Do you have an efficient call structure?
- Do you have an objective method for comparing candidates?
- Do you know what information you will share with the hiring manager once completing the call?

If you can't answer yes to all the above questions, then you're simply not ready to make the call.

Let's look at what actions you need to take:

- Describe what makes a candidate worth considering?
- Define when you are going to schedule the calls
- Describe your call structure
- Describe how you will compare candidates, what is the criteria?
- Describe how and what information you will provide to the hiring manager?

Once you've done this, you can then look at who and how to engage:

- Define who is involved at the various steps in telephone interview process, (organisation, attending etc)
- Define your engagement strategy with potential candidates (what and how will do you do it?)

And now that you've done all this, what are the benefits of preparing for your initial calls in this way?:

- What are the general benefits of defining a telephone interview structure?
- What are the benefits to you in doing this?

- What are the benefits to your hiring manager in doing this?
- What are the benefits to potential candidates in doing this?

And there you have it, a very simple yet powerful way of making sure you are prepared for your initial conversations with candidates.

The initial conversation

I was taught that the main objective of the initial call should be that the candidate should be in a position where, by the end of the call, the candidate will verbally commit to accepting an offer of employment, if after the recruitment process is completed, the role presented matches all of their requirements!

Now it's not always possible to get this commitment at such an early stage in the process, so there are three other clear objectives you should be aiming for:

- Commitment of their interest in the role
- Permission to send their details to the hiring manager
- Commitment to attend interviews

A well-defined call structure will enable you to achieve all these points, and help you deliver feedback to the hiring manager.

You've got a defined call structure, right? It's important to go into every call with a structure in mind, but be flexible, play with it, have fun!

I have a call structure and I'll share it with you now

Call Structure:

1. Introduction
2. Current Situation, Skills and Experience
3. Needs and Motivation
4. Clarification
5. Presenting & Selling the opportunity
6. Closing Candidates
7. Asking for Referrals
8. Building a Relationship

The call structure is pretty flexible although the one thing you really can't change in terms of the order, is the introduction, it would be weird to start a call without introducing yourself wouldn't it? Believe it or not, some recruiters are so eager to get their message across in a call, they completely forget about introducing themselves!

Let's look at each step.

Introduction

The introduction is your chance to make a great impression. Your candidate might be busy, particularly if your headhunting and don't have a pre-arranged time for the call. You might only have 30 seconds to impress!

What should you include when you're making your introduction?

First, you should ascertain that you are actually talking to the person you want to speak to!

We've all been there, excited to be calling a prospective candidate, starting talk at 200 miles per hour, only to find out after 30 seconds or so, you're talking to your candidate's mum or dad!

A simple, "Hello, am I talking to……?", will avoid this awkward situation.

Ok, so we've got the person on the other end of the line, how are we going to introduce ourselves and what do we need to cover in this 30 second to one-minute pitch?

Let's assume you've already been in contact over email and you've booked a call for a certain time with the candidate. What would you say?

Did you cover the following?:

Your name? Your position? The company you work for? The reason for your call? Is it still convenient to talk?

If you didn't, then your introduction failed. Why? A candidate will want to know who you are, what you do, the company you work for and the reason for the call. Despite the fact they may have applied for your role; in the time between them applying and you booking your initial conversation with them, they may have been in touch with 3, 4 5 or more companies about opportunities, and if you don't tell them the basics in your introduction, they'll be wondering who you are, which company it is and which role it is you wish to talk to them about. It becomes an awkward situation.

They're confused and you've probably got a bad impression of them because you think they're unprepared.

Another key thing about your introduction is? Yes, that's right, your pitch and tone.

You should be confident, relaxed, enthusiastic and personable when you call your candidates. Nobody wants to pick up a call and hear a recruiter the other end who sounds like they just got out of bed and this call is going to be an effort!

If you're not happy and engaging when you make the call and present yourself in your introduction, you've already lost the candidate.

TIP: Smile and dial, people can hear when you're smiling and talking and feel the effect.

What's next?

A lot of recruiters make the mistake of jumping straight in to presenting the opportunity. They are so desperate to tell the candidate about the job, that they go straight in to pitching the role, going through all their selling points, telling them about the salary and benefits and…. The candidate is not interested! Shit, what went wrong?

It's boils down to one of the most basic principles of sales – You can't sell someone something they don't need or want.

This means you should adopt a need based selling approach and to do that, you need to find out as much about your prospect and their needs, in order to understand how to sell your offering to them.

Current situation, skills and experience, achievements

This is the part where you can find out the information zou need to understand if the person matches the key requirements of the role in terms of skills and abiliities, mixed with experience.

You've had an excellent briefing with your hiring manager, and you know what they want to see in your feedback, so that must mean you know what questions you're going to ask, right?

I find it's always good to to break the ice by getting the candidate to talk about their current situation before you start asking about their skills and abilities, experience and achievements. I like to ask something like "Tell me what's happening with you right now, why are we talking?". It's a nice soft question that should help the individual open up an account of their current status and feel calm and relaxed while doing so.

I also make sure at this stage, that I get an understanding of their status in other other job applications, so that I can compare the opportunities in the needs based selling later on in the call, hopefully showing them why our opportuity is the best one for them.

I'll then ask just a few questions about the skills and abilities, their experience and achievements, because I've always planned what questions I need to ask, to get the information I want to know that also meets the hiring managers expectations in terms of feedback.

Needs and Motivations

Gathering the candidate's needs and motivations, listening to them and showing you've understood is probably the most important part of the call. It's important because as I mentioned early, without it you will not be able to sell your opportunity to the candidate.

So what do we define as needs vs wants?

It's simple, a need is a 'must have' where-as a want is something 'nice to have' You need to apply this train of thought and really differentiate between the them.

For examples, most candidates will say they'd like a salary of xx, that's what they want. So you could respond with, "ok so how negotiable are we on that?", or if you know you're not able to meet their level (because in some companies there are salary bands and pay groups which are company-wide and can not be changed), then you can be open and say

"I'm afraid I can't meet your current expectations, if you were willing to negotiate, what's the lowest you'd accept?" The lowest is more likely to be what they need.

Now I want to make a point here. You will see some so called 'Influencers' on LinkedIn stating it's not acceptable to ask a candidate what they expect, and that this tactic is used purely to try and get the candidate as cheap as possible. That's absolute bollocks!

This isn't about driving candidates down on their salary request. It's about understanding if you can pay them what they want, or whether there is room for negotiation. If there's not. It's an opportunity to be straightforward and honest and tell them that you can or cannot meet their needs and avoid wasting their time discussing the opportunity further.

What candidate needs do you think you need to understand?

I'm not answering that for you, I want you to think about that however, if you get stuck, I provide training on this and if you want to get deeper in to it, you'll have to pay me to come and educate you.

When we talk about candidate motivations, I like to stick with the theme of money and use sales people as a general target group that inherently believe they should say they are motivated by money when asked in interview what motivates them. It's down to you to understand you are only scratching the surface if you do not dig deeper.

When I get salesperson who tells me this, I push back. I tell them; "everybody tells me they're motivated by money and I don't believe really believe that, tell me why you're motivated by money?"

The candidate then usually tells me about what they can do or what they can buy with the money.... there's your real motivation! The money is simply a tool, it's what they can do or buy that motivates them.

When you ask a candidate what motivates them, you're likely to get the standard answers about progression, rewards, training and development and others. If you do, ask why what they have told you motivates them, then you get to understand what their real motivations are.

So now I've clarified that for you, you're ready for the next stage.

Clarification

You've asked the questions you need to ask to understand your candidates needs and motivations. It's important to follow up and clarify that. When you clarify that you have understood your candidate's needs and motivations, it shows them you have listened to them and it makes them feel important. It's also important because it can bring out other needs and motivations that the candidate may have forgotten to mention to you.

It's simple and I shouldn't need to go into it in detail, so I won't. Essentially, you can tell the candidate that you want to be sure you've understood them, and repeat back to them everything they've told you Asking if that's correct. If it's not, gather the new information, clarify it again and hopefully you get it covered.

Now you know everything you need to know about your candidate, you've got to think quickly and decide if the opportunity you have matched their needs and motivations.

If it doesn't, you need to be honest with the candidate and tell them that based on what they've told you about themselves, the role isn't going to be right for them. Trust me, they'll thank you for your honesty and for not wasting their time further. They'll also be more likely to be interested in talking to you in the future because...?

Becasue you took the time to get to know them, understand them and were open and honest with them.

If you think the role is a good match for them, it's time for you to sell!

Presenting and selling the opportunity

Presenting and selling the opportunity is easy if it matches your candidates needs. You simply position the opportunity in a manner that matches the needs, demonstrating how it matches their needs.

The other point to remember here is you are selling! Yes you are, don't argue with me, if you believe your not selling, you're in the wrong job!

When you present the opportunity, you need to present it in an enthusiastic, engaging manner that will get your candidate excited about it. You should be showing your passion for the company and as well as showing the candidate how the opportunity and company meets their needs, giving them your own personal reasons and examples of why the candidate should join your company.

Remember the 'smile and dial' comment earlier? Well this is where you really should be using it!

Imagine you went shopping for a new mobile phone, you walked into the mobile phone shop, excited about getting the latest samsung galaxy or apple i-phone (I didn't want to discriminate :)) and you're greated by a slaes person who sighs, turns around to quickly speak to their colleague, comes back to you with a fake half-smile and clearly doesn't want to be there. Your experience isn't going to be that great is it?

At the same time, don't over-egg it! Be aware that if you tell someone it's ‚AMAZING or FANTASTIC' you need to justfy why it's amazing or fantastic.

So, you've sold your soul and the candidate seems excited about it, let them ask questions and do your best to give them any further information they need.

Now it's time to close your candidate

Closing Candidates

Can you remember the main objective of the call and the three other objectives?

If you can't, you need to go back a few pages and read about them again....ok, only joking, let's get to it!

The first stage of closing is to get commitment of their interest in the role. Simply ask the candidate, "How interested are you in this role?" If you've done a great job on you call so far, they should confirm they are interested in the position.

Ask them if they have any concerns or doubts about the opportunity.

If they highlight a potential concern (raise an objection), it's back to needs gathering and clarification for you, to help you understand if you missed anything. Once you fully understand the concern, demonstrate how that concern can be overcome (overcoming objections) and then ask the candidate if that solution would work for them. If it doesn't, you need to dig deeper. If it does, fantastic, move to the next step.

You need to send your feedback along with the candidate's profile to the hiring manager. Confirm that you want to share their details with the hiring manager and ask for their permission to do so.

I can't imagine that any candidate who is interested in the position would say no at this point, but stranger things have happened!

It's important to close the candidate in advance for interview dates and time. Confirm that they are willing to attend video face to face interviews. You can do this by simply asking, "I assume you'd be happy to attend an interview with the hiring manager?". Again, I'd be very surprised if they said not at this stage and would begin to question the rationale behind it.

Assuming the candidate has agreed, I'd then ask them for dates, times and ensure I have plenty of flexiblity to select a time that is suitable for the candidate. You have to remember that not everyone has enough holidays to take time out for interviews (especially if they are in the hiring process with a few companies) and many people are uncomfortable with throwing a sickie to be able to attend interviews. You need to allow for flexibility in your process. It's also important at this stage to inform them how many steps there are, whether there's any testing involved, what format the interviews will be and how quickly they can expect the whole process to run.

Finally, if you've covered all the above, try your luck, ask them; „If the interviews went well and the role described and the people and company met your expectations, and we came back to you with a suitable offer, I presume you'd be happy to accept it?"

The same as before, if the candidate shows any sign of heistation or is unsure, Ask them if they have any further concerns or doubts about the opportunity. It might bring up something unexpected, if not, then it's likely they just don't want to commit right now...

Asking for referrals

Asking for referrals is something that I've found external recruitment agents are far better at than internal recruiters.

I don't know why internal recruiters don't ask for referrals when talking with potential candidates on the phone. Perhaps they feel it's more polite or professional to wait until a candidate they have spoken to becomes an employee? Perhaps they're worried it might seem inappropriate? I'm really not sure, but here's my take on it.

I might have multiple roles I am recruiting for, and I might be facing a shortage of talent. I don't think it's rude to ask towards the end of a call „I've got a lot of other roles on at the moment, do you know anyone else who I might be able to help secure a new career opportunity?".

It's clear from that that I am not asking the candidate to recommend someone for the role I have just spoken to them about, that really would be poor practise.

I don't think it even matters if it's a call with a candidate who you're moving forward with or not. If you've built good rapport with them, and they feel you're someone they can trust and would potetnially talk to in the future, they will recommend you to their friends and colleagues who might be looking for a new role, and this could provide you with the needle in the haystack you've been looking for.

Ask for referrals on every call, what's the worst that could happen? The candidate might say sorry I don't know anyone...

Building Rapport

I'm not sure whether you're born knowing how to do it or whether you can learn it, but building rapport with your candidates is essential in gaining trust and commitment from them.

A lot of recruiters will feed back on candidates with comments such as; "We had a great conversation, he/she has a great personality and we joked a lot, we built a strong relationship on the phone"

Now, it may well be that they did build a strong relationship, but building rapport is not about telling jokes and having a laugh, there's much more to it.

Rapport can be defined as ,an emotional connection and mutual understanding between two people'.

Rapport can happen naturally, where two people instantly 'hit it off' or get on well without having to try – they have shared experiences and much in common. In other circumstances, it can be developed consciously by finding some common ground and demoonstrating empathy.

It can be difficult to build rapport with candidates, they can be nervous and on their guard, you might not have a connection with them in any form at the very start, but thr great thing is that rapport can built throughout the conversation.

Here's a few tips:

- Be polite and use small talk to break the ice
- Use active listening to uncover experiences you can relate to, which could give you more to talk about
- Try to use humour, but don't make jokes about other people, joke about yourself or situations you've encountered
- Demonstrate empathy, show the candidate you understand their point of view/feelings
- Use the candidate's name frequently during conversation
- Calrify answers and provide feedback
- Openely agree with the candidate if you do, and explain why
- Be honest and admit if you do not knwo the answer to a question raised by the candidate
- Be genuine, don't try to play the professional recruiter persona, be human and be yourself

The initial call is not difficult as long as you have a good structure and have planned your questions in advance. It can be flexible too.

I was advised many times that a recruiter must lead the initial call with a candidate. I don't believe that's true. I believe a recruiter must drive the call to ensure both parties get what they need from the conversation, but the order in which the recruiter approaches the call can be flexible, especially in cases where senior/experienced candidates can be quite strong personalities and can demand / want to know information before telling you about themselves. Would you really want to push back and say no? If you would, then take a moment to think about how being combative and argumentative is going to have an impact on that candidate and their experience.

Interviews – The Horror of it All

Interviews.... aren't they bloody awful!

They needn't be, but generally they are. It's the most nerve-racking part of the whole process for candidates and yet many organisations, whether small or large, tend not to think about that and provide experiences that are bloody awful in terms of their poor preparation, lack of professionalism, rudeness and more.

I've got several horror stories myself from my own experiences as a candidate and in all cases but one, I decided to withdraw from the process because of the experience.

For me the candidate experience during the interview process begins from the moment you have confirmed you'd like to invite them for interview. Everything from this point on must be well organised, run smoothly and be as much of an enjoyable experience as possible for the candidate.

NOIB*ing* can help your hiring team manage this crucial stage, let me show you how.

In the same way we prepared for the pre-screening we need to F.A.E.B. We'll look at the **Facts**, what **Actions** we will need to take, how we will **Engage,** and then visualise the **Benefits**

So, how do we do it? Well first off, let's consider the facts:

- Have you schedule time in your calendar for interviews (assuming you are attending)?
- Have you schedule time with the candidate and the hiring manager?
- Have you booked adequate facilities and equipment for the interview?
- Have you agreed on the format of the interview with the hiring manager?
- Do you have an efficient interview structure?
- Do you have an objective method for comparing candidates?
- Have you agreed how and when you will discuss feedback with the hiring manager?

If you can't answer yes to all the above questions, then you're simply not ready to hold the interview.

Let's once again, look at what actions you need to take:

- Describe how and when you will schedule time for the interviews
- Describe the facilities / equipment you will need and use for the interviews
- Describe what your format and interview structure will be
- Describe how you will compare candidates objectively
- Describe how and when you will discuss feedback with the hiring manager

Once you've done this, you can then look at who and how to engage:

- Define who is involved at the various steps in F2F interview process
- Define your engagement strategy with the hiring manager
- Define your engagement strategy with potential candidates

And now that you've done all this, think about what the benefits are, of preparing for your interviews in this way:

- What are the benefits of being well prepared for interviews?
- What are the benefits of defining an interview structure?
- What are the benefits to you in doing this?
- What are the benefits to your hiring manager in doing this?
- What are the benefits to potential candidates in doing this?

And there you have it, again very simple way of covering the basics, and making sure you are on your way to being prepared for your interviews with candidates.

But, there's more! Let's dig a little deeper into the different stages of the interview cycle to really get under the skin of where a lot of companies are getting it wrong.

The interview invitation

With the exception perhaps of manual / factory floor workers, most companies confirm interviews by email and/or outlook appointments.

What a great opportunity to further engage with your candidate and enhance their experience.

Generally, I've found that an interview confirmation will contain the following information:

- Date
- Time
- Location
- Who you will be meeting with
- What to bring with you
- Contacts on the day in case of any problems
- A short line to wish me luck

And that's about it…. Inspiring eh?

There's so much more that could and should be done with this interview confirmation. Here's just a few suggestions:

Location; send a map or even better, a link to directions on google maps. Make it easy for your candidates to plan their journey and find your offices.

The hiring manager(s).... send links to their online profile(s) or include a short biography about them with a picture, so the candidate can see in advance who they are going to meet. Putting a face to a name will help them in feeling more comfortable.

Send them the job description. Whether they applied to your advert, or you headhunted them direct; you've told them about the role, now let them see it in writing so that they can take on board the information and come to the interview better prepared.

Tell them about the format of the interview. Help them get prepared. It's in your best interests for them to perform well at the interview stage.

Inform them about next steps that may occur if the interview goes well for both parties. Help them understand what will happen and the timescales to help manage their expectations.

Include links to videos of your employees or provide links to social profiles and pages belonging to the company that really show of your brand. Keep them excited about the possibility of joining your company.

I could provide more suggestions, but then there'd be nothing left to educate you about when you invite me to train your hiring team, so that will do for now.

Post Invitation Follow Up

How often have has there been an occasion where you've been ghosted by a candidate? They haven't arrived for their interview and you can't seem to get hold of them. Day's pass and you've had no response to your calls or emails asking if everything is ok because you're now concerned if they are still alive!

This can be avoided, not always, but most of the time. As a recruiter the phone is your best friend you should use it regularly for communication with your candidates.

Surely you understand the importance of calling a candidate a day before their interview date to see if they are prepared and whether they have any last-minute questions.

Of course, as well as being in a position where you genuinely want to help make sure they do their best on interview, it's really a smoke screen for ,Are you still coming tomorrow?'. Doing this by phone is far more effective than by email and it's far better to find out now, rather than when a hiring manager calls you advising their interviewee hasn't arrived, sending you into a panic, scrambling around for the phone number and then surprise, surprise, not being able to get hold of the 'missing person'.

Preparing Reception

When I say preparing reception, I don't mean physically going to clean it, although it might not be a bad idea if it looks a mess, hey someone's got to do it!

What I actually mean is that whoever is working on your reception desk (or if you work in a shared office or workplace, whoever works on the main reception), should be told in advance of your candidate's arrival and should be prepped to greet them with a smile, acknowledge that the hiring manager(s) is expecting them, and offer them tea, coffee, water or an opportunity to use the rest rooms.

I'll tell you about my most entertaining experience in this regard. I once went for an interview with a large international company. I had received my interview confirmation and had checked out where I needed to be and how I was going to get there. I arrived early and parked the car and arrived at the security gates.

To my horror, I suddenly realised there were multiple entrances on site, and I hadn't been advised which entrance to report to. At the third attempt I found the right one. Unfortunately, no-one advised me that that the security guards did not speak English. Luckily, I had printed my interview confirmation, so I showed them the paper. I had to sign some papers; I had no idea what I was signing but at least I was directed to reception.

When I arrived at reception I spoke to the receptionist (who did speak English) and told her who I was there to meet. She advised me to go and sit down 'over there' and my interviewer would be with me shortly.

Over there, was two rows of dirty, old chairs facing each other across a table that had leaflets and brochures strewn all over it. Strewn all over the chairs were a group of factory workers who were either on a break or had just finished their shift and I'm sorry, but they stank! Ah…. the sweaty stench of body odour combined with the aroma of steel, how delightful.

No water, no coffee, no tea, no idea where the rest room was, and 20 minutes sat in a chair watching hundreds of people pass by, looking at me looking at them. To cap it all, that 20 minutes I was waiting took the delay in interview start time to 15 minutes past the time it should have started.

What an experience! I expect better, and so do your candidates.

Meeting & Greeting

You've been there haven't you? Sitting patiently, nervously waiting for your interviewer(s) to come and great you. And the moment arrives. First impressions count, don't they?

A lot is made about candidates that arrived interviews behaving in an unprofessional manner. I'd argue the same could be said for recruiters and hiring managers too. I like to categorise them and have a few favourites.

The Juggler:

The Juggler is usually an internal recruiter. They come bundling through the door using their elbows because both hands are full. They've usually got a laptop, paper and pen, the candidate's resume and their mobile phone balanced on one hand, and in the other their pint mug of coffee!

As they come to great the candidate, they attempt to balance the coffee precariously on their laptop so as to have a free hand to shake their hand.

They ask the candidate to follow them to a meeting room, once again managing to fill both hands with all their crap, leading them through a series of doors, each one opened either with their elbow, or by awkwardly leaning over with a pass they now carry in their mouth. They seem to enjoy shoulder charging each door and do so until they've reached the door to the meeting room, which they lean against beckoning the candidate to enter the room ahead of them, despite leaving only a small amount of room. The candidate passes by sucking in their stomach nervously staring into the eyes of the recruiter as they pass in the hope they don't accidently bump into that mug of coffee or the laptop.

Elsa, Queen of Arendelle:

Elsa of course is the Queen of Arendelle from the movie Frozen (just so happens to be one of our favourite films, of course referring to my two daughters Natalka and Valentyna). Regardless of gender, there's many recruiters and hiring managers who seem to pull off this persona with ease.

The candidate has arrived at reception and the receptionist is lovely, he's smiling, he's offered them water, shown them where the rest rooms are, and he's called the recruiter or hiring manager to let them know they've arrived.

Suddenly, there's a cold chill in the air, the windows are frosting up and the receptionist has put his jumper on. The door swings open and as the snow drifts in, here's the interviewer, dressed sharply, gliding across the icy floor towards the candidate, with a face looking like they've just sucked a lemon.

They confirm the candidate's name and if the candidate is lucky, they tell them their name, Elsa, and they quickly ask the candidate to follow them. The walk is long, it seems like endless, dark corridors with no windows, no pictures, and there's no words spoken between the interviewer and the candidate. It feels colder and colder, darker and darker as the candidate almost falls over their feet trying to keep up behind icy Elsa, as she strides with purpose towards the icy room in which they're about to experience the most unfriendly and impersonal interview they've ever had.

Elsa flings open the door and asks you to take a seat, then advises she's going to get the hiring manager and will be back in a moment. No offer of tea or coffee whilst you sit and wait in a room that feels like it hasn't been heated for millennia. Your left contemplating whether this is all just a bad dream…

The Secret Agent:

The Secret Agent often stealthily creeps into reception; they look smart but unassuming. They're looking around as if to check out the exits and methodically assess every individual present in order to understand who they'll have to assassinate first. It's as though they're ready for some serious corporate espionage.

As they glance at the candidate, the candidate looks at them expectantly hoping to maintain eye contact…. but the secret agent turns away. They pick up some papers on the reception desk and look at them intensely, the candidate is beginning to wonder if it's some sort of hitlist and whether their name is on there. They begin talking quietly to the receptionist and the candidate can't hear what they're saying, perhaps it's a secret message. Are they a secret agent? No, surely they're simply a different employee?

The candidate turns their attention to something else in the reception area, they've focused on the magazine on the table in front of them and just as they pick it up…. Holy shit, the secret agent is standing beside them! They have a silver pen in their hand and the candidate isn't if it's secretly a James Bond type laser gun or some form of poison filled capsule that they're going to inject into the side of their neck, putting them to sleep before they interrogate them like a captured spy.

Thankfully, they great the candidate with a big smile and confirm their name, introduce themselves and offer to take them to the meeting room where they'll have the interview. The candidate follows them but can't help noticing the camera's as they pass through grey walled corridors. They're on their guard, ready to escape at any point should their suspicions be found to be true…

The Whirlwind

I love the whirlwind! These recruiters absolutely crack me up. It's as if they've been at their desk snoozing, daydreaming the day away, and that call from the receptionist advising them the candidate have arrived, has put them in a state of frenzy.

It generally starts with the recruiter or HR person crashing through the door. They must have just sprinted from the other side of the building because they're out of breath (and in summer months often sweating profusely too) and almost doubled over as the inhale huge gulps of air.

They come to great the candidate, shaking hands with their sweaty palms, and talking at them so fast, you could forgive the candidate for thinking they'd just become a judge at a speed talking championship. Regardless, the candidate listens attentively and understands the recruiter needs to go and find the hiring manager and has asked them to wait in reception a moment.

Whoosh, they're off, spinning, crashing and banging their way out of reception and off down a corridor that the candidate can only assume leads to a labyrinth of offices where they need to hunt down the hiring manager.

A few minutes pass and smash, bang, wallop! The reception door slams open, the recruiter is sprinting through and shouts at candidate as they pass, "Be with you in a moment".

A few moments later, they're back again, beads of sweat running from their forehead. They come to candidate, and almost as if all their breath has gone, they croak, "I've found them", grimacing at the obvious discomfort they're in.

But wait it's not over, the candidate is encouraged to follow the recruiter to the meeting room, and my god it's the fastest they've ever moved through a building. The candidate notices a few ceiling tiles out of place along the way and can't help wondering if the whirlwind was the cause.

There are other personas for sure; there's those who despite having arranged the interview, are completely unprepared, others who have no understanding of time and are late, and then there's others who greet candidates professionally and appear to be human, engaging candidates in conversation, making them feel a little less nervous, and trying their best to create as good an experience as possible for everyone.

I simply want to state, first impressions really do count. Make the most of your opportunity to create a welcoming environment for your candidates when they arrive for their interviews.

Dependant on your company style, I think it's only fair that if you dress in a certain way, you should make this known to candidates in your interview invitations and invite them to dress in the manner that suits that.

Who Should Recruiters Report To?

In many businesses there's not much though given to who the recruiters / recruitment team should report to, simply because it's seen as part of the overall HR function. It goes without saying then, that it would make sense to have the them reporting to an HR Director, right?

I want to make one thing really clear at this point. If you have a recruitment team which has a recruitment manager leading the team. That manager should be on a par with the HR Manager due to the specialist skillset, experience, and value they add to the business. They should therefore not report into the HR Manager (Cue all the HR Manager precious about their little empires howling in disbelief that I would say something like that).

Don't get me wrong, I've worked with great HR Managers and have worked very well in partnership with them. I don't make this comment just to get an effect. I make this comment because your recruitment leader is a partner for your business, much in the same way as your HR Manager, albeit offering advice, guidance and support in different areas.

I've worked in a variety of roles, in both small and large businesses, where I have reported either to the VP HR, directly to business owners or to the VP Operations. I've had good experiences in all cases however, my personal preference was the role in which I reported directly to the VP of HR, Why?

The VP of HR in question was a lady called Marjolein Grijsen. To put it simply, she was one of the best leaders I ever worked with.

I feel this way because when working with her, I felt she supported me, shared her knowledge, coached me and I feel I gained much experience from her during my time working with her.

She empowered me to make my own decisions and run recruitment the way I felt would best serve the needs of the business. She also gave me direct access to the business leaders with whom I would attend regional and sometimes global conference calls, not just to simply provide information, updates and reports, but also to provide advice in workforce planning and future hiring etc.

Marjolein made me feel like I was empowered to do my best for the business.

It's your call as to who you want your recruiters / recruitment team to report in to but ultimately, I firmly believe that if the person delegated responsibility for recruitment, empowers the recruitment function and enables its performance, it shouldn't matter who the direct reporting line is.

Turf Wars

Firstly, you need recognise that Recruitment (or Talent Acquisition) professionals are different from HR professionals, albeit they are one of the many different functions that sit within HR as a general organisation that covers many areas.

In general terms, Recruitment Professionals are responsible for candidate attraction and management of the recruitment process. They may often work with HR to define organisational needs, create job descriptions and design hiring plans, but unlike HR professionals, Recruiters need to be able to wear many different hats such as Marketing, Sales, Coach and Psychologist.

Recruiters have strong people skills and a solid understanding of tools and technologies needed to find candidates. They enjoy selling and matchmaking and want to maintain a high level of candidate and hiring manager interaction, it's quite unlikely that they are going to want to do HR related tasks.

An HR professional, has most likely studied for qualifications in an HR related field and has a broad knowledge of employment law, they actively participate in many / all areas related to onboarding, employee engagement, talent management, reward and recognition, training & development, disciplinaries, payroll, comp & bens and more, right through to off-boarding. In some smaller companies, they will also manage the recruitment process.

I do believe, regarding working environments, recruiters need to be, and should be, separated from HR professionals.

Imagine the scenario:

You have a large office, there's a group of HR administrators, T&D specialists and HR Generalists, Payroll, C&B and Admin, and in the corner there they are, the recruiters.

They're really fucking noisy! Oh my god! They're always on the damn phone talking; if they're not on the bloody phone, they're on skype or zoom calls and if they're wearing headphones that's even worse, for some reason they seem to talk even more loudly!

They have daily stand ups in their corner discussing recruitment stuff with each other every damn morning while the other team members in the office are trying to drink their coffee in peace! They have fun, they enjoy their work and they're performing well BUT, it's distracting, and the 'real' HR pros are getting annoyed. They can't concentrate with all that noise. They're feeling more and more frustrated daily.

It starts to become a problem, someone in the T&D team has approached the recruitment team lead to state it's too noisy and they can't concentrate.

What can the Team Lead do? The business hasn't got enough meeting rooms for the team of recruiters to do their screening calls in private. The Team Lead tries to compromise by taking the morning meetings upstairs into the canteen, away from the HR Pro's. Actually, it's great, there's a choice of breakfast and more coffee and biscuits, and there's comfortable seating areas too, so perhaps that's not a bad thing anyway; BUT, the calls continue, and they will continue as it's an essential part of the role.

Meanwhile, the HR administration team have now joined forces with the T&D team and have complained to the HR Director. This time however, the complaint is not just about the noise, apparently the recruitment team are having too much fun and it's like a wild animal sanctuary!

The HR Director has a little 'chat' with the recruitment team leader, he/she doesn't mention anything about the great morale in the recruitment team and the better than expected performance (in fact a record quarter compared against the last two years), he/she focuses only on the complaint about things being a little wild, asking the team leader to resolve the situation.

The recruitment team leader doesn't understand, it's not wild, it's a team that has bonded well, that enjoys what they're doing, has fun whilst doing it, and performs excellently, the team has a culture and everyone in the team is enjoying being part of the team in that environment. The Recruitment Lead becomes disengaged, he/she doesn't consider the working environment viable, he/she resigns. Along with him, other key members of the recruitment team resign, leaving the business trying to fill the gaps left with inexperienced staff from the HR function in the hope that business continuity won't be affected………

Ok, so it's a little bit of fun, mixed with some truth from my own personal experience. Unfortunately, it does happen. So how do you avoid the headache of warring factions?

It's simple. Prepare an office or space in which the recruitment function can be themselves. Give them an environment in which they can perform the essential tasks involved in recruiting, without being frowned upon for doing it. Sitting them in an open plan environment together is great, but don't mix them with finance, HR or other operational teams.

You don't need to fear about the team feeling separate from the business, or closing themselves off, if they have their own space. Good recruiters will regularly 'floor walk' to say hello to other people, get a feel for what's happening internally and to see and feel the culture of other teams they are recruiting for........and of course catch up on any office gossip!

Close

To be honest, I never thought I would ever write a book, but as I was writing this book, I grew more and more passionate about it and I believe every word I say.

This section should have something poignant, something important to say, but I haven't got anything left to say on the basics.

I thought long and hard about whether to go really in to detail and start writing about 'candidate engagement' or start providing training on many different facets of the recruitment process, but I figured the book would lose its essence, and I might not ever get a chance to provide training to recruiters, HR professionals or hiring managers again if I included everything. It would also probably take me a year to write it!

Writing this book has been a refreshing change for me. In the 6 weeks it took me to write this book, I've been through the highs and lows of feeling like I am getting somewhere, to having writers block and sitting staring at the screen for two days solid, deleting and re-typing the same sentences over and over.

The worst part of it was the moment I had a little too much to drink and decided I would write some more at midnight one Saturday evening, It was rather foolish and I carelessly managed to delete 5 weeks' worth of work, and was not able to recover the document.

The best part of it, was when I sat down after wanting to die, and a light bulb went off in my head. I realised I have all the information in my head and could re-write it easily. Even better was the renewed vigour and focus, that helped me realise the first version was absolutely shit, with my mind wandering off in many different tangents. This book now says everything, and only the things I wanted to say.

Will there be a follow up? You bet your arse there will! It might take a little longer, as I start a new internal recruitment role in January 2020 and I need to start preparing for that now, but there'll definitely be two more books. One focused on the minefield that is recruitment strategy, one focused on internal recruitment team management, and one focused on all the bullshit surrounding candidate engagement. Shit, that's three, I never was good at maths!

Thank You

I'm going to get a little sentimental here. I owe a few people some thanks, and this just feels like the right time to put it in writing, so here we go.

Jean-Christoph Baudais – Thank you for believing in me. Thank you for making me laugh and thank you for putting this stupid fucking idea into a reality and pushing me to get it done. I hate you. Ok, I love you really, but for the love of god, when are you ever going to take me out for dinner in Paris you mean old git!

Marjolein Grijsen – You were simply the best! Thank you for helping me become what I am and thank you for becoming a client later in our careers too, it's been a pleasure and you're always in my thoughts.

Iain Pike – A good friend but you were never any good in supplying me with candidates! You tricked me into becoming your business partner for a few years, reeling me back in when I wanted to go off and do the next hairbrained idea I had. If it wasn't for you, I'd be rich! Ha-ha, ok, so thank you for investing and taking time to deal with my somewhat all or nothing personality. I'm not bi-polar, honest!

Kevin Smith – I owe you a great deal Kevin. You're too fucking smart for your own good! I hate that I could never win an argument with you. I'm grateful for the opportunity you gave me, and I learnt more in a few years with you, than in most of the twelve or thirteen years prior to that. I hope you continue your success.

Pierre-Olivier Landry – Another French person on the list, I must be turning more and more European in my mindset. I always remember our interview and the one line that sticks in my head. You said, "I can't work out if it's just British bullshit or whether you really are as passionate as you seem to be about recruitment!" I hope I proved it was the latter. It was fun working with you.

Lenka Haskova – You were never my manager, thank god! But you provided me with a great deal of support, sometimes professionals, sometimes personal and sometimes during difficult periods. One of the best HR Manager's I've ever worked with. I'm happy to be able to call you a friend, even after all these years.

There's a lot of other people who are probably worth a mention, but I don't want to turn this into a love fest. To everyone I've ever worked with. To colleagues and friends who I've been a leader for over the years, thank you all.

THE BIGGEST THANK YOU is reserved for my partner in life and mother of my two beautiful daughters, Jitka. You are everything to me and without you, none of this would ever be possible. You drive me, sometime into delirium and madness, but more importantly, to all the small successes I've had in my professional life. You don't often understand what I do, and usually can't believe how I manage to do anything at all, but you're always there and this means the world to me. I love you.

Finally

I hope you've enjoyed reading this little book about the basics of internal recruitment. I hope it achieved what I set out to do which is to challenge your thinking and get you to start thinking and acting in a different way when it comes to the recruitment journey.

As per the Looney Tunes cartoons…. that's all folks

Paul

Printed in Great Britain
by Amazon